Photo credits:

Stanley Breeden/DRK — Page 27
Fred Bruemmer/DRK — Pages 11, 24
John Cancalosi/DRK — Pages 25, 29
Chuck Dresner/DRK — Front Cover; Page 8
Michael Fogden/DRK — Pages 6, 11-13, 16, 20-22, 24-25, 27
Stephen J. Krasemann/DRK — Page 27
Wayne Lynch/DRK — Page 20
James P. Rowan/DRK — Front Cover
Belinda Wright/DRK — Pages 6, 9, 16, 23, 27
John R. Patton — Pages 6, 14
A.B. Sheldon — Pages 6, 14, 17, 21, 23
Nathan W. Cohen/Visuals Unlimited — Pages 7, 15, 17, 29
John D. Cunningham/Visuals Unlimited — Pages 7, 24-25
C.P. Hickman/Visuals Unlimited — Page 22
A. Kerstitch/Visuals Unlimited — Page 11
Joe McDonald/Visuals Unlimited — Pages 8, 13-14, 21, 26, 28-29
Jim Merli/Visuals Unlimited — Front Cover; Pages 7, 14-15, 17, 23, 26
Ron Spomer/Visuals Unlimited — Page 10
Milton H. Tierney, Jr./Visuals Unlimited — Page 27
Breck Kent — Front Cover; Pages 7, 9, 12-13, 17, 23, 25, 28-29
John Giustina/Wildlife Collection — Page 9
Martin Harvey/Wildlife Collection — Page 10
Jack Swenson/Wildlife Collection — Pages 8, 15
Dan Suzio — Page 25
Tom McHugh/Photoresearchers — Page 27

Illustrations:
Robin Lee Makowski — Pages 18-19

EYES ON NATURE™

SNAKES

Written by
Jane P. Resnick

kidsbooks®
Incorporated

SO MANY SNAKES!

There are so many different kinds of snakes! In the 100 million years they've been on Earth, snakes have developed into 2,700 species. These slender reptiles come in many colors and sizes. A really big snake can grow to over 30 feet and weigh more than 300 pounds! And while the vast majority are harmless to humans, some snakes are deadly.

FABULOUS FANGS

When most people picture a snake, they see FANGS. But only poisonous snakes have fangs. Some serpents, like rattlesnakes, have fangs that fold against the roof of the mouth, hidden but always ready to strike.

The fangs of the rough-scaled bush viper.

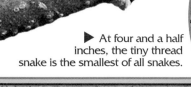

▶ At four and a half inches, the tiny thread snake is the smallest of all snakes.

▲ Pythons are the largest snakes.

▲ Basking in the sun helps keep a snake warm.

COLD LIKE A LIZARD

All snakes are reptiles. (Scientists who study snakes are called *herpetologists*, which comes from the Greek word *herpeton*, for reptile.) Like lizards—their closest relatives—snakes are cold-blooded. Their temperature depends on the air around them. If they are exposed to too much heat or cold, they will die. About 70°-90°F is ideal. Although found almost everywhere, no snakes can be found in icy polar regions.

▲ A kingsnake shedding its skin.

NEW SKIN

All their lives, snakes grow, but their skin doesn't grow with them. As the skin gets tight, the snake starts to shed. First, the skin coloring becomes dull. Even the scale covering the eye, called the *spectacle*, turns white. Then the snake rubs the skin off its nose and wiggles out.

The scale pattern and spectacle are easy to see in shed skin.

SCALE TALE

Scales make the snake. They completely cover a snake and are part of the skin, which is smooth and satiny—not slimy. A special pattern of scales on the head identifies species. *Dorsal scales* cover a snake's back. On the belly are *ventral scales*, also called abdominal plates, which grip the ground as the snake moves.

SLENDER FELLA ▶

Snakes may not have legs but they have ribs—as many as 400. This long, flexible spine is the reason they can twist and turn and move on the ground and on trees. A snake has a body and a tail. All a snake's organs are narrow and line up end to end in its skinny body.

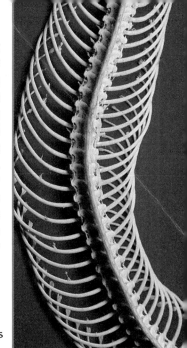

▼ This corn snake demonstrates how flexible its spine really is!

7

ALL IN THE FAMILIES

Besides the things they have in common, snakes have characteristics that set them apart. That's why there are eleven families of snakes. Those families with the most species, or kinds of snakes, are the boas and pythons, cobras and coral snakes, vipers, and typical snakes.

▼ The South American anaconda.

▲ One boa beauty is the emerald tree boa.

RAINBOW SKIN

Boas can be big, but they can also be small—and beautiful. Just look at the rainbow boa. This four-foot snake from Central America and northern South America has an unusual shining quality. Although only rusty brown with dark rings, the boa shimmers with color.

Rainbow boa

BIG BEASTS

In the boa and python family you'll find the largest snakes. What's big? In order to go eyeball to eyeball with the biggest ones, you'd have to climb three flights of stairs and look out a third story window! The anaconda (a boa) is nearly the longest (about 30 feet) and certainly the heftiest (over 330 pounds). It is found mostly near the water, preying on South American crocodiles called caimans.

8

◀ SWAYING SNAKES

The cobra family is a poisonous one, and contains many kinds of cobras, coral snakes, mambas, kraits, and sea snakes. Fast and graceful, the Indian cobras are famous for spreading their ribs and raising themselves off the ground.

▼ Northern copperhead

The Australian death adder is often mistaken for a viper, but it's in the cobra family.

VIPER SNIPER

Vipers, which include rattlesnakes and copperheads, are found all over the world, except in Australia.

PYTHON HEAVEN

Pythons are found in many places, but Australia and the nearby Pacific islands is a region rich in these snakes. D'Albertis' Python (below) is found only in Papua New Guinea.

TYPICAL TYPES

The family of typical snakes dominates all regions of the world, except in Australia— where the cobra reigns. There are over 2,000 species in this group, out of the total 2,700 kinds of snakes! It's one big family, and it includes the harmless ratsnakes, corn snakes, kingsnakes, and garter snakes, as well as the poisonous boomslang, twig, and keelback snakes.

These corn snakes demonstrate how snakes can differ even within a species. One is *normal* (far left), another *melanistic* (has so much pigment that it's black), and the third is *albino* (lacking pigment in its skin).

9

WHERE THE SNAKES ARE

Snakes are specialists. They have behaviors suited to their *habitats*—the places where they live. And because they are cold-blooded, they adapt their behavior to the climate. Snakes in hot, dry regions seek cool, moist places underground. Snakes in cool areas hibernate in dens when it's cold.

▲ A western rattlesnake finds a neat nook in the rocks to keep c[...]

▲ A sidewinding adder buries itself in the sand to escape the hot sun.

DESERT DWELLERS

Snakes are super desert survivors because their tough skin keeps them from drying out. Most desert dwellers need shelter from the heat and are only active at night, dawn, and dusk. Some, like the horned viper (right), have hornlike structures to keep sand out of their eyes and to protect them from the sun. Imagine! Serpent sunglasses!

UNDERCOVER

"Burrowing" snakes live in burrows and are sometimes mistaken for worms. Short and cylinder shaped, they are toothless and eat worms and insects. They barely have eyes. The burrowing blind snake family has 200 members, none of which are more than 10 inches long. Not actually blind, they can see just well enough to get around in the dark underground.

Western blind snake

ng, and these garter snakes are
ng from their den.

NG A BALL

akes that live in cooler
ates hibernate when tem-
tures drop. Their heartbeats,
athing, and growth slow
wn so much that they
barely alive. They
this for just a few
eeks or up to eight
onths—in a den.
akes of different types
ibernate together. They
url together to conserve heat,
ometimes forming a "ball."

The yellow-lipped
sea krate.

SURPRISING SWIMMER

They don't have flippers or fins, but snakes can swim. Snakes that live in the sea almost never leave the water. They have a paddlelike tail, which helps them swim, and they can stay underwater for a long time, possibly hours. Members of the cobra family, sea snakes have very potent venom.

TROPICAL PARADISE

A tropical forest is a snake's dream—with plenty of places to live. There's a floor for land rovers and rich earth for burrowing types. Also, there are trees, where a snake uses its tail like a monkey to hold on to limbs. Many snakes blend in with leaves or branches. Some, like the oriental whip snake (right), have a pointed snout so both eyes can look straight at an object—a fast-moving lizard or bird—and catch it.

▲ The fierce fer-de-lance is at home in the rotting tree stumps of the South American forest.

11

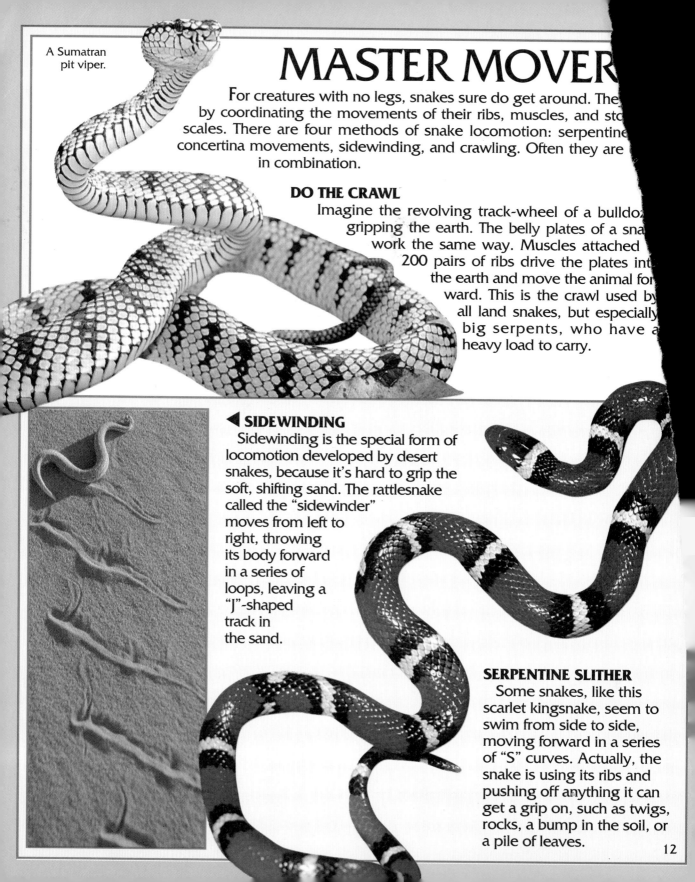

A Sumatran pit viper.

MASTER MOVER

For creatures with no legs, snakes sure do get around. The[...] by coordinating the movements of their ribs, muscles, and sto[...] scales. There are four methods of snake locomotion: serpentine[...] concertina movements, sidewinding, and crawling. Often they are [...] in combination.

DO THE CRAWL

Imagine the revolving track-wheel of a bulldo[...] gripping the earth. The belly plates of a sna[...] work the same way. Muscles attached [...] 200 pairs of ribs drive the plates int[...] the earth and move the animal for[...] ward. This is the crawl used by[...] all land snakes, but especially[...] big serpents, who have a[...] heavy load to carry.

◀ SIDEWINDING

Sidewinding is the special form of locomotion developed by desert snakes, because it's hard to grip the soft, shifting sand. The rattlesnake called the "sidewinder" moves from left to right, throwing its body forward in a series of loops, leaving a "J"-shaped track in the sand.

SERPENTINE SLITHER

Some snakes, like this scarlet kingsnake, seem to swim from side to side, moving forward in a series of "S" curves. Actually, the snake is using its ribs and pushing off anything it can get a grip on, such as twigs, rocks, a bump in the soil, or a pile of leaves.

12

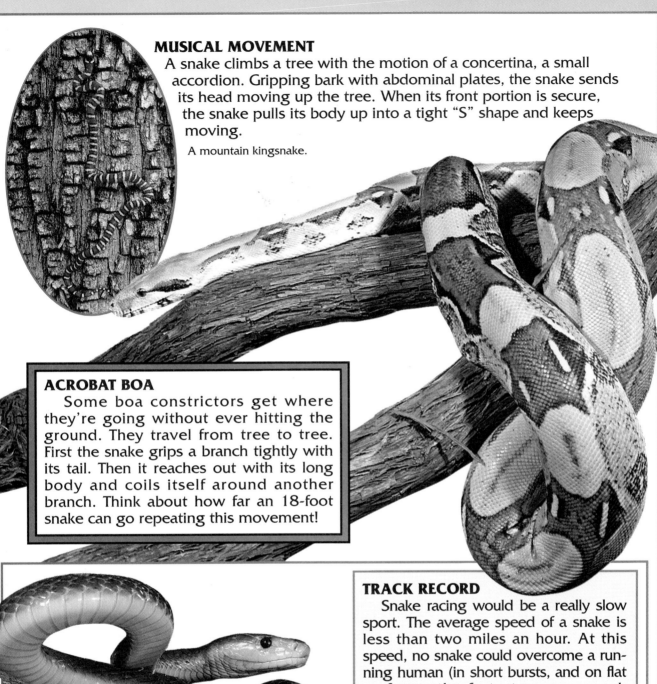

MUSICAL MOVEMENT

A snake climbs a tree with the motion of a concertina, a small accordion. Gripping bark with abdominal plates, the snake sends its head moving up the tree. When its front portion is secure, the snake pulls its body up into a tight "S" shape and keeps moving.

A mountain kingsnake.

ACROBAT BOA

Some boa constrictors get where they're going without ever hitting the ground. They travel from tree to tree. First the snake grips a branch tightly with its tail. Then it reaches out with its long body and coils itself around another branch. Think about how far an 18-foot snake can go repeating this movement!

TRACK RECORD

Snake racing would be a really slow sport. The average speed of a snake is less than two miles an hour. At this speed, no snake could overcome a running human (in short bursts, and on flat surfaces, the fastest runners reach speeds close to 27 miles per hour). But where there are rocks, bushes, and uneven footing, a snake could easily slither faster than a person chasing it.

◀ In eastern Africa, it is said that the black mamba can move at 10 to 12 mph and chases people aggressively.

13

SNAKE SENSE

Smell is a snake's most powerful sense, but not so much through the nostrils as through the forked, flickering tongue. The tongue picks up microscopic particles from the air and ground. Because it is forked, the tongue can pick up a scent from more than one direction at a time—left, right, down, up, straight ahead, and all directions in between. With this ability, the snake can zero in on its prey.

▲ A rattlesnake smelling an intruder.

◀ A kingsnake sniffing a trail.

▲ SNAKE SIGHT

Even if a snake's eyes are wide open, it doesn't see very well. Like this gaboon viper, most have eyes set on either side of their head, and they can't focus. But they can see when something moves. Prey animals have a better chance of escaping a snake if they stand still.

◀ EYE OPENER

No creature stares like a snake. Just look at this bush viper! Snakes have no eyelids, so they always appear to be staring, even when they're sleeping! The clear lens known as the spectacle, which is one of the snake's scales, protects the eyes. Under this shield, a snake's eyes moisten and move, and stare and stare.

▼ SNAKE EYES

The pupils of a snake's eyes are a telltale sign of its activities. Those snakes with round pupils travel during the day. These are called *diurnal* snakes. Snakes with pupils the shape of an oval slit from top to bottom are night, or *nocturnal*, hunters.

▲ The pointed shape of the vine snake's head helps it see straight ahead. These two daytime hunters seem to be working as a team!

This tree boa is a night hunter.

IT'S THE PITS

What do water moccasins and rattlesnakes have in common with pythons and boas? Pits! Facial pits are sensitive to heat. They help the snakes locate warm-blooded prey, especially at night. With pits between the eye and the nostril, a viper can "feel" a passing mouse and strike accurately, even in total darkness.

Note the pit of this eyelash viper!

GOOD VIBRATIONS

Snakes have no outer ears to spoil their smooth outline. But they do have an inner ear. They "hear" you coming by sensing vibrations on the ground through their jawbone, which sends the signals through connecting bones to the inner ear and brain.

15

A BIG APPETITE

Snakes eat meat, and that makes them *carnivores*. They kill three ways: They seize prey in their mouth. They squeeze with their coils. Or they poison prey using deadly fangs. Smaller species dine on insects, worms, lizards, and frogs. The largest species can swallow mammals the size of a small deer.

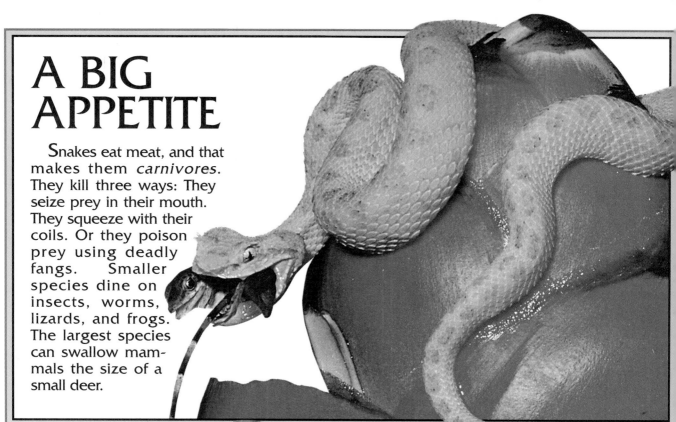

▲ An eyelash viper eating a lizard.

DON'T FORGET TO BREATHE!

When a snake eats, its mouth is completely filled. Even its air passage is blocked. How does it breathe? Its breathing tube slides forward to create an opening (left). Also, the tongue slides back into a little pocket. Meanwhile, saliva pours into the mouth to make the prey slide through the jaws easily. And backward pointing teeth dig in to keep even slippery frogs from escaping.

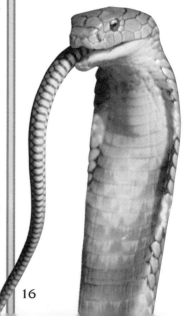

▼ Like the kingsnakes, this king cobra is named "king" because it makes a meal out of other snakes. It's also the longest venomous snake in the world.

16

JAWS!

What can you fit in your mouth? Not much compared to a snake. A snake cannot chew or bite off pieces. It swallows its food whole—and usually headfirst. The secret is in the jaws. The lower jaw unhinges so the mouth opens WIDE. Also, the lower jaw has two separate halves connected by elastic tissue. The snake works one side and then the other, until the victim is swallowed.

STRIKE. YOU'RE OUT!

Vipers are the master predators of the snake world. When they strike, the fangs unfold, shoot directly forward, and stab the victim, filling it with poison. The snake then pulls back to avoid being injured. The poisoned victim usually runs away, but the venom slows it to a full stop, and the snake tracks it down.

THE BIG SQUEEZE

Pythons, boas, and their relatives really know how to squeeze the life out of prey. These *constrictors* grasp prey in their mouth and coil around it. They constrict, or squeeze, the prey until it can no longer breathe and the heart stops.

HARDLY HUNTERS

Most snakes don't hunt. They usually wait for prey to come to them. But some do go looking for food. There are also snakes that "fish." Like the copperhead above, they use their tail as "bait," luring prey into close striking range.

IN DIGESTION

A snake is so slim you can watch a meal travel to its stomach, pushed by strong muscles moving in waves. Digestion takes several days or even weeks, depending on the feast. Powerful stomach juices dissolve everything but hair and feathers. If the next meal is hard to find or the snake is hibernating, the snake can go for months without eating.

17

POWERFUL POISON

Say "poisonous" and people think snake! But of the approximately 2,700 snake species only about 400 are poisonous, and fewer than 50 are dangerous to people. Most poisonous snakes avoid human contact if possible. Some don't even live close to large populations of people. In fact, the largest and possibly most dangerous snakes cause few human deaths because they mostly live in remote areas. These big snakes include the king cobra, black mamba, taipan, bushmaster, eastern diamondback rattlesnake, and gaboon viper.

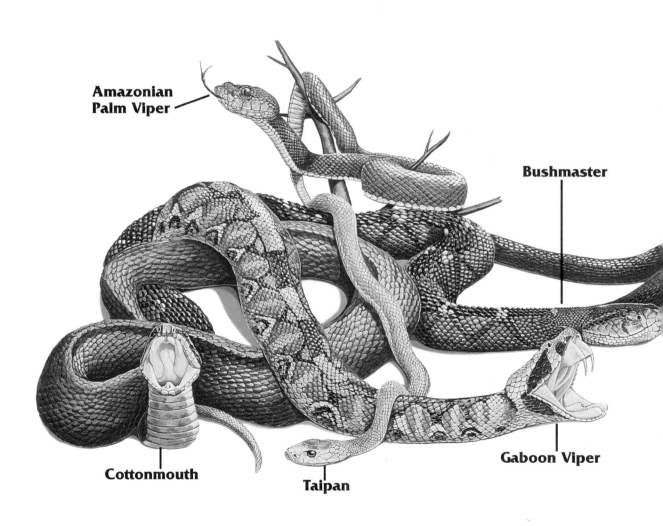

Amazonian Palm Viper

Bushmaster

Cottonmouth

Taipan

Gaboon Viper

All poisonous snakes are dangerous if encountered. Their venom acts on blood or nerves. Some venom does both. Viper venom acts on the nerves, whereas cobra venom acts on the blood. Cobras probably have the most potent venom. The king cobra has brought down elephants. Just one teaspoon of its venom could kill over 65 people.

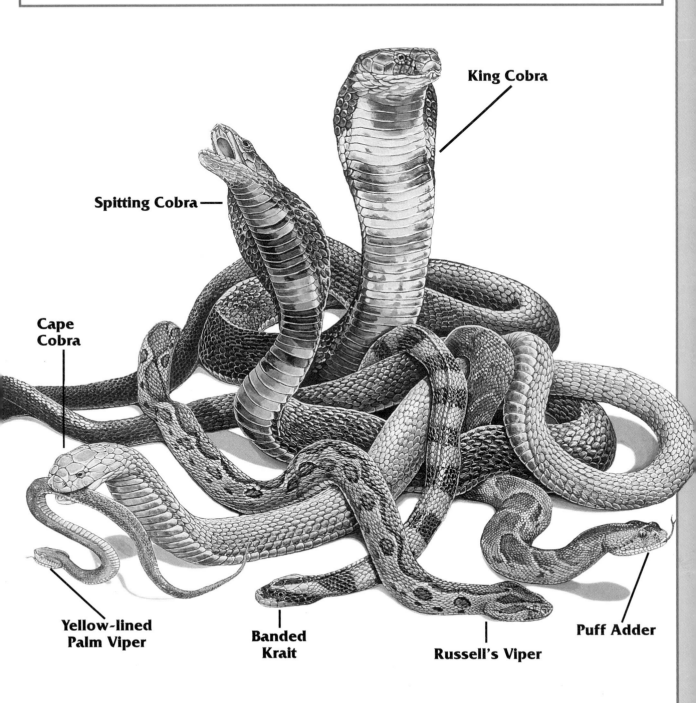

King Cobra

Spitting Cobra

Cape Cobra

Yellow-lined Palm Viper

Banded Krait

Russell's Viper

Puff Adder

DEFENSE !

Snakes have enemies. Mongooses, roadrunners, secretary birds, and serpent eagles specialize in eating snakes. Raccoons, owls, coyotes, and others find them a good meal, too. Hiding is a snake's first line of defense. Scaring or intimidating an enemy works for some. Distracting is another measure. The ultimate maneuver is biting.

BACK OFF!

The rattlesnake uses several defense methods to tell an intruder to get out of its way. The snake may hold its forked tongue out stiffly. It may raise its body in the air. And it may rattle its tail. The noise of the shell-like rings on its tail is an alarming sound and would probably be enough to stop you in your tracks. It is said that the rattle can be heard from over 160 feet away!

A prairie rattlesnake about to strike! ▶

This twig snake puffs up to frighten enemies.

PUFFED UP

To a snake trying to scare away an intruder, being bigger seems better. The puff adder gets its name from puffing itself up to face an attacker. The snake expands its ribs so it looks larger and scarier than it is. The cobra is known for opening its hood. For added effect, the spectacled cobra has a scary mask on its hood.

HISSSSS! ▶

Snakes are silent because they have no vocal cords. But some do hiss to warn invaders. The bull snake is one of the loudest. A very thin membrane in the front of its throat makes the sound possible. The snake opens wide and blows hard against this membrane. The vibration causes the nerve-shattering hiss.

A spectacled cobra.

▼ SURPRISE!

Surprise is a good defense method and there are snakes who like to startle their enemies. The water moccasin has the nickname "cotton-mouth" because it opens a gaping white mouth to frighten intruders.

▼Opening the mouth is one defense tactic many snakes use.

SPITTING COBRA ▶

The African black-necked cobra spits poison to defend itself, and it can hit its mark from eight feet away! The snake raises its head, takes aim, and sprays venom through pinholes in the front of its fangs. Contact with the poison can cause eye damage or even blindness.

A bandy bandy from Australia, raising its body as a warning! ▼

SNEAKY SNAKES

Snakes have some pretty sneaky ways of fooling their enemies. Some have a built-in way of hiding called *camouflage*. Their skin color or pattern blends in with their surroundings. Some other tricky tactics include *mimicry* and *death-feigning*. Mimicry is when a non-poisonous snake has taken on the look of a poisonous snake.

NOW YOU SEE IT... NOW YOU DON'T!

Snakes use all kinds of ways to disguise themselves. The green vine snake (above) hangs motionless in trees and looks like just another vine. The puff adder has a skin pattern that breaks the outline of its body so that it disappears among its surroundings. The twig snake has a head shaped like part of tree.

Puff adder

Twig snake

HEADS OR TAILS ▼

The sand boa has a blunt tail that looks amazingly like its head. When threatened, this snake ducks its head, coils tightly, and sticks up its tail. Enemies mistakenly attack the tail. The sand boa knows a scarred tail is better than a squashed skull.

▲ The poisonous coral snake.

COLOR SHOCK ▲

Ringneck snakes blend in with their surroundings when they're on their stomach. If trouble comes near, they hold up their colored tail for shock effect. If that doesn't scare the trespasser, the snakes roll over on their back and really blast their enemy with color.

The harmless kingsnake. ▲

COLORFUL CORAL

The poisonous coral snake is small (about 3 feet), shy, and pretty. It's ringed with red, yellow, and black. So are a lot of harmless snakes. They are mimicking the dangerous coral snake so that predators will think twice about striking them. If you ever see a red-yellow-and-black snake, remember: Red touch yellow, kill a fellow. Red touch black, poison lack.

PLAYING POSSUM

If a predator should come around, the hognose flattens out its head and hopes to look scary. If this fails, the hognose "dies" right before the predator's eyes. It twitches and twists as if it is in pain and breathing its last breath. Then the snake flops over on its back, opens its mouth, and lets its tongue hang out. It may even peek to see if the enemy is gone before flopping back on its belly and crawling off.

SNAKES ALIVE!

▲ An eyelash viper mother and her newborns.

Imagine giving birth to 50 babies at one time. Boa constrictors do. They and many other snakes give birth to live offspring. Other snakes lay eggs. Some, like the reticulated python, lay 100 or more. After laying eggs or giving birth, most mothers, but not all, take off.

SHE'S MINE!

Reproduction begins with a snake's sense of smell. A scent trail leads males to females. Sometimes it may lead to a wrestling match if another male is around. With rattlesnakes, like the ones to the left, there is a "combat dance." The male snakes raise their body high into the air and push against one another. But they never bite. One finally falls over and slinks away. The other finds his mate.

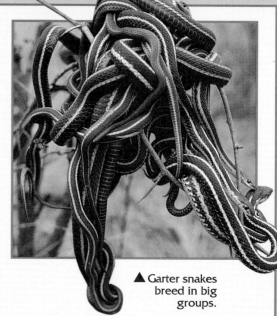

▲ Garter snakes breed in big groups.

MATING GAME

When mating, a male and female entwine their two bodies and stay together for a few minutes or several hours.

24

HOT SPOT

A female laying eggs takes great care in finding a nesting spot that will provide shelter, moisture, and warmth for her eggs. In burrowed holes, beneath stones, and among rotting leaves are fine places.

MOTHER WARMTH

The Indian python is one of the few snakes that "sits" on her eggs. After pushing the 50 to 100 eggs into a pile, she coils around them, resting her head on top. Then she contracts her muscles to raise her body heat and warms them.

▼A corn snake laying eggs.

TOUGH STUFF

Snake eggs are tough, not brittle like birds' eggs. They are leathery, soft, and flexible. The eggs start out oval and grow, changing shape as the snake inside develops. The snakes hatch by poking their way out with an "egg tooth," a kind of horn on their snout that breaks off after this one use.

▼A hog-nosed viper giving birth.

◀ LOOK ALIKE

Most baby snakes are miniature copies of their parents. Take a look at this boa constrictor and her newborn. Baby snakes may be colored and patterned differently. But some change as they develop and end up looking exactly like their parents.

SMART SNAKES ▶

Because there are no adults to care for them, young snakes must catch and kill their own food. At birth, they must be totally equipped to survive. Venomous snakes have sacs full of poison and fangs ready to use. As you can see from this newly hatched pine snake, babies are fully aware they must protect themselves.

25

DARING TO BE DIFFERENT

A two-headed snake.

▲This pink kingsnake is an albino.

Some snakes really stand out from the crowd. These distinct creatures may be different from other snakes in the way they behave—how they move, reproduce, or eat. They may live where most other snakes could not. Or, they may just look incredibly unusual.

REPTILE RHINO ▶

Hornlike formations do not seem very snakelike, but the rhinoceros viper of Africa has them. This serpent has a blue-and-yellow butterfly design. Its nickname is the "river jack" because the rhinoceros viper is found near streams and rivers.

EGGS ON THE MENU ▼

The African egg-eater chooses eggs for every meal. Big eggs. Opening its mouth incredibly wide, this serpent can swallow an egg twice as thick as its own body. As the egg moves down its throat, the snake pierces it with a sharp spine. The contents travel to its stomach, but the snake spits the shell out.

SOLE MATE ▲

Usually, it takes two to make babies, but there is one snake that does it all alone. The female Brahminy blind snake will not wait around if she can't find a mate. Her eggs will develop on their own, and her babies will all be female.

SNAKE OR FAKE? ▶

Is it just a weird snake or what? If so, where's its tail? Actually, this creature is a caterpillar from the rainforest in Costa Rica. By mimicking a snake, it hopes to frighten away predators.

TRAPEZE ARTIST

The "flying snake" is the acrobat of the snake family. Found in southern Asian countries, often in trees, this three-foot snake travels branch to bush to ground by flattening its body and *gliding* down. It lands with the greatest of ease. But it can't "fly" back up. It must crawl.

The tentacled sea snake, also known as the fishing snake, lives in Southeast Asia.

The elephant's trunk snake is totally aquatic.

UNDERWATER SURPRISE

There are plenty of snakes that live in the sea, in lakes, or in rivers. Most of them look like snakes. But some look so unusual, they might fool you into thinking they're not snakes at all!

27

SNAKES AND US

Snake charmers fascinate their audience and the snake! The snake isn't charmed by the music, though. It is watching the swaying movement of the piper.

Today, when you say "serpent," many people think of the biblical story of the garden o Eden. But snakes have represented many othe things besides evil, such as wisdom, death, an love. The Greeks saw snakes as a symbol c immortality—not that snakes live forever, bu they do shed their skin to become new again.

Southern Pac
rattlesn

ROYAL SNAKE EATER▼

When people find kingsnakes in their yard, they leave them alone because these serpents kill other snakes—even deadly rattlesnakes. A constrictor, the king grabs the rattlesnake behind the head and coils around the prey's body. The king is immune to the rattlesnake's venom, so very often it goes unharmed.

RATTLESNAKE ROUNDI

Snakes are not the only ones that wear the skin. People make shoes, bags, and clothes c of snake skin. People also kill snakes for spo What used to be a rattlesnake hunt in colon times is now a roundup in which thousands snakes are killed in a single weekend. As ma as a half-million may be killed each year, most them western diamondbacks.

DON'T TREAD ON ME

In the United States, where there are 15 species, rattlesnakes really get people's attention. The majestic 8-foot eastern diamondback is the largest. During the Revolutionary War, colonists chose this viper as a symbol because it doesn't attack unless threatened, it warns its victims, and it's fearless when struck. Flags flew with the snake's image and the words "Don't Tread on Me."

2

FARMER'S HELPER

A rat snake is a welcome sight to farmers. These snakes eat the rats and mice that destroy crops in grain stores. The corn snake may be the prettiest, but the yellow rat snake actually seems to enjoy people. As a pet, it's often found in the house curled up in a pot or drawer.

SNAKE MEDICINE

The venom that poisons people is also used to make medicine. "Milking" snakes for their venom is done by holding their head and pressing, which causes the venom glands to squirt. The venom is used to make antidotes that erase the effects of the poison. The venom of vipers is also being used in medicines to treat high blood pressure, heart failure, and kidney failure.

PLAY MATE

Keeping a snake for a pet can be fun—and very interesting. Harmless North American snakes are best. Snakes like boas grow too big—in three years a baby boa could be five-feet long. A good snake house is an old aquarium or glass-fronted box with a mesh top. Snakes also need water, food, and kindness—like any other animal.

he endangered ndigo snake.

Although gentle, this gigantic Burmese python might not make the best pet. Where would you put it? And what would you feed it?

DISAPPEARING SNAKES

Some snakes are disappearing from the Earth because their habitats are becoming places for roads and houses. In the United States several snakes are endangered: the indigo snake of the Southeast, the ridge-nosed rattlesnake of southern Arizona, the Atlantic salt marsh snake of the eastern Florida coast, and the beautiful San Francisco garter snake.

San Francisco garter snake